SandCastle™

Let's Measure

WHAT
in the
WORLD
is an
INCH?

Mary Elizabeth Salzmann

Published by ABDO Publishing Company, 8000 West 78th Street, Edina, Minnesota 55439.
Copyright © 2009 by Abdo Consulting Group, Inc. International copyrights reserved in all countries.
No part of this book may be reproduced in any form without written permission from the publisher.
SandCastle™ is a trademark and logo of ABDO Publishing Company.

Printed in the United States of America, North Mankato, Minnesota.
012009   072011

Editor: Pam Price
Curriculum Coordinator: Nancy Tuminelly
Cover and Interior Design and Production: Colleen Dolphin, Mighty Media
Photo Credits: Colleen Dolphin, Shutterstock
Illustrations: Colleen Dolphin

Library of Congress Cataloging-in-Publication Data

Salzmann, Mary Elizabeth, 1968-

What in the world is an inch? / Mary Elizabeth Salzmann.

   p. cm.

ISBN 978-1-60453-166-4

1. Length measurement--Juvenile literature. 2. Measurement--Juvenile literature.

3. Weights and measures--Juvenile literature. I. Title.

QC102.S343 2009

530.8'13--dc22

                 2008005484

SandCastle™ books are created by a professional team of educators, reading specialists, and content developers around five essential components—phonemic awareness, phonics, vocabulary, text comprehension, and fluency—to assist young readers as they develop reading skills and strategies and increase their general knowledge. All books are written, reviewed, and leveled for guided reading, early reading intervention, and Accelerated Reader® programs for use in shared, guided, and independent reading and writing activities to support a balanced approach to literacy instruction. The SandCastle™ series has four levels that correspond to early literacy development in young children. The levels are provided to help teachers and parents select appropriate books for young readers.

SandCastle Level: Fluent

Emerging Readers
(no flags)

Beginning Readers
(1 flag)

Transitional Readers
(2 flags)

Fluent Readers
(3 flags)

SandCastle™ would like to hear from you! Please send us your comments or questions.

sandcastle@abdopublishing.com

www.abdopublishing.com

An inch is a unit
of measurement.
A U.S. quarter is
about an inch wide.

← 1 inch →

Inches are used to measure the size of something. When you know how big an inch is, you can find out how big things are.

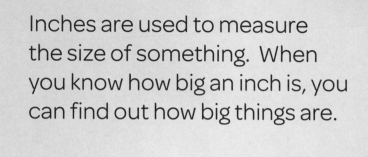

The symbol for inch is ".
1 inch is the same as 1".
12 inches = 1 foot

tape measure →

ruler →

Rulers, yardsticks, and tape measures are tools you can use to measure inches.

20 21 22 23 24 25 26 27 28 29 30 31 32 33 34 35 36

MADE IN USA

yardstick

KEVIN CAN MEASURE!

Kevin measures his napkin.
It is 5 inches long.

5"

Kevin measures his
glass of orange juice.
It is 7 inches tall.

7"

Kevin measures his celery sticks.
Each celery stick is 3 inches long.

3"

He uses his celery sticks
to measure his plate.
The plate is 9 inches across.

(3 celery sticks = 9 inches)

Kevin shares his brownie
with his friend Claire. He breaks
the brownie into two pieces.

2"

2"

Then Kevin measures the pieces. He makes sure they are the same size.

Each piece is 2 inches wide.

Kevin makes a sandwich for
his little brother to take to school.
He measures the sandwich to
see what size container he needs.

5"

5"

6"

6"

Then Kevin measures the container to see if it is the right size for the sandwich.

MEASURING EVERY DAY!

Kayla measures how deep the sandbox is. It is 8 inches deep.

8"

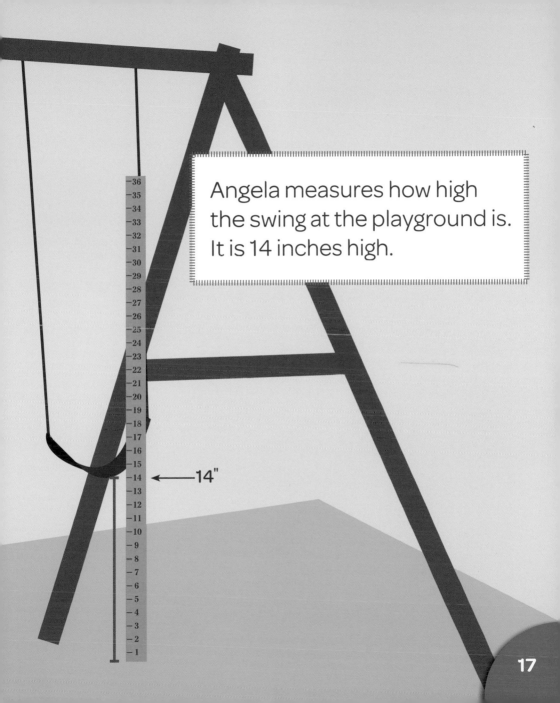

Angela measures how high the swing at the playground is. It is 14 inches high.

14"

Eric measures a tree in the park. The tree trunk is 30 inches around.

30"

Alex measures the distance between his bed and the bedroom door. The bed is 75 inches from the door.

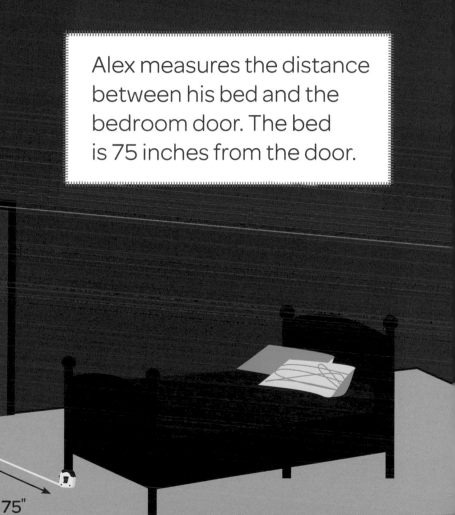

75"

MEASURING IS FUN!

How many inches is your favorite toy?
What else can you measure in inches?

LET'S MEASURE!

Which of these things is about one inch?

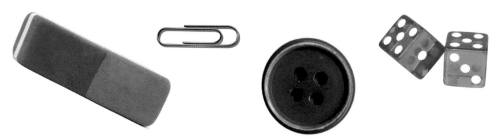

(answer: button)

MORE ABOUT MEASURING

Length

12 inches = 1 foot

Sometimes you use both feet and inches to measure something.

2'6"

The table is 2 feet and 6 inches wide. This can also be written 2'6".

GLOSSARY

container – something that other things can be put into.

distance – the amount of space between two places.

favorite – someone or something that you like best.

measure – to determine the size, weight, or amount of something.

measurement – a piece of information found by measuring.

ruler – a tool used to measure length.

share – to divide something between people or take turns using something.

unit – an amount used as a standard of measurement.

yardstick – a measuring tool that is one yard long and marked in inches.

899